The Insignificant Woman

Kimberly Moses

REJOICE
Essential Publishing

Kimberly Moses/Rejoice Essential Publishing

PO BOX 512

Effingham, SC 29541

www.republishing.org

The Insignificant Woman/ Kimberly Moses

ISBN-13: 978-1-952312-47-2
Library of Congress Control Number: 2021930664

Dedication

This book wouldn't be possible without the inspiration of the Holy Spirit. During the Covid-19 pandemic, the Lord had me revisit a teaching that He gave me for a women's conference in 2019. I expounded on it. As a result, this book is the fruit of my fellowship with the Lord.

2 Timothy 3:16-17 says, "All scripture is given by inspiration of God, and is profitable for doctrine, for reproof, for correction, for instruction in righteousness: That the man of God may

be perfect, thoroughly furnished unto all good works."

Contents

ACKNOWLEDGMENTS.......................................v

INTRODUCTION..1

CHAPTER 1: Abigail.............................5

CHAPTER 2: Abishag..........................12

CHAPTER 3: Achsah............................19

CHAPTER 4: Bilhah.............................24

CHAPTER 5: Dinah.............................28

CHAPTER 6: Elisabeth.........................32

CHAPTER 7: Eunice And Lois............35

CHAPTER 8: Euodia And Syntyche........................38

CHAPTER 9: Hagar.............................42

CHAPTER 10: Jael.................................47

CHAPTER 11: Jehosheba........................50

CHAPTER 12: Joanna..............................53

CHAPTER 13: Jochebed.........................56

CHAPTER 14: Junia.................................60

CHAPTER 15: Keturah............................63

CHAPTER 16: Lydia.................................66

CHAPTER 17: Persis, Tryphena, And Tryphosa................70

CHAPTER 18: Phoebe.............................74

CHAPTER 19: Priscilla............................78

CHAPTER 20: Puah And Shiphrah.........................81

CHAPTER 21: Sheerah............................84

CHAPTER 22: Tabitha 87

CONCLUSION: The Story

Acknowledgments

I WANT TO THANK ALL the members of my YouTube membership. You guys supported and believed in me when the Lord opened up a new avenue to create new content. You guys are awesome.

I want to thank all my ministry partners, supporters, mentees, spiritual daughters and sons. Thank you for all the prayers and support.

I want to thank my husband for allowing me to write and go forth in my calling.

I want to thank the Edmonds for always being available to pray for me when I encounter warfare.

I want to thank my parents, siblings, family, leaders, and those who encouraged me throughout this journey.

Introduction

ARE YOU FEELING LEFT out or rejected? Well, you aren't alone. Around the world, many women feel the same. Perhaps someone has made you feel small, unimportant, powerless, or meaningless. In essence, they've deemed you as insignificant. There are women in the Bible that are considered insignificant. We rarely hear about them or know nothing about them at all. When we think about women in the Bible, certain names come to us, such as Ruth, Ester, Mary, or Deborah. These were great anointed women, but what about the ones who God used powerfully, but are rarely mentioned?

Have you been considered insignificant? People may have counted you out, but God has counted you in. People may have forgotten about you, but God says that He will never leave nor forsake us. People may have rejected you, but God accepts you. People have tried to curse me, telling me that I would never become anything in life, but God said otherwise.

Imagine being anointed and overlooked. God called me into ministry in 2014. I didn't get my first speaking engagement until two years later. Most people would've quit, but I continued to press. After that, opportunities came sporadically but never consistently. I knew that I had the fire of God upon my life and that I would do something great for the Lord one day. However, in the natural, things looked bleak. I didn't understand why others seemed to experience promotion but not me. The Lord had to show me that there is something special inside of me and never to compare myself with others. What God has for me is for me. I learned to get busy for God and have tunnel vision, only focusing on Jesus. I didn't have time to worry about what God was doing in someone else's life or ministry. Everything will happen at an appointed time.

Are you feeling discouraged because of a lack of support? Don't get caught up in numbers. Zechariah 4:10 says, "Don't despise the day of small beginnings." I remember only having four people watching my videos. Now, I have thousands of views. It didn't happen overnight, but I remained faithful. I appreciate the process and know that God gets all the glory. I can recall when I felt frustrated because I was considered insignificant or a "no name." When you are a "no name," it seems like no one will listen to you or give you the time of day. Keep preaching anyways. If the seats are empty, preach like you are speaking to the masses. Eventually, God will bless you for your faithfulness and those empty seats will be filled. You must continue to speak what God has given you because it's awesome and someone needs to hear it. People may not want to listen to you now, but things will change in your favor. God is the best promoter and will open up doors that no one can shut. God can give you influence and He can give you a voice that is heard.

You are important. It doesn't matter what anyone thinks about you. If God is for you, then it doesn't matter who is against you. You are the apple of God's eyes. One of my uncles tried to curse me when I was young. He said that I would be pregnant by the age of twelve, but the Lord said otherwise. I didn't get pregnant until I married. One of my High School teachers said that I would never accomplish anything in life. The Lord made sure that every word curse fell to the ground. He will do the same for you. Why? Because we matter. We were created for a purpose and we are His daughters. God loves us more than we can ever know. Remember, the women who are considered insignificant in the Bible are His masterpiece just like us. There was a purpose for why God created them. Let's look at their lives and discover their importance. They were special to God, just like you. Let their qualities empower and encourage you along your faith journey.

1

Abigail

ABIGAIL WAS THE WIFE of Nabal. After his death, she became the wife of King David. Her name means the father's joy.[1] Her name has a prophetic meaning because she brought God, the Father, joy. Just as she brought the Lord joy, you do as well when He looks down upon His beautiful creation. We can read about her story in 1 Samuel 25. Nabal, whose name means fool[2], was a difficult person. He was mean, harsh, and very selfish (verse 3). He was wealthy and wouldn't help others in need. King David and his

1. "H26 - 'Abiygayil - Strong's Hebrew Lexicon (KJV)." Blue Letter Bible. Accessed 18 Oct, 2020. https://www.blueletterbible.org//lang/lexicon/lexicon.cfm?Strongs=H26&t=KJV
2. "H5037 - Nabal - Strong's Hebrew Lexicon (KJV)." Blue Letter Bible. Accessed 18 Oct, 2020. https://www.blueletterbible.org//lang/lexicon/lexicon.cfm?Strongs=H5037&t=KJV

men needed food and supplies, but Nabal was very harsh with them (verse 10-11). As a result, he put his family and the men who worked for him in danger because David and his men were about to attack (verse 13). However, Abigail moved swiftly and gave food and supplies as a peace offering (verses 18,35).

Having summarized Abigail's story, let's look at the following characteristics that she possessed:

- Dealing with difficult people
- She saved lives
- Wisdom
- Quick thinker, moved swiftly
- Discerning
- Beautiful

Have you ever had to be around someone difficult? Perhaps they were mean, demonized, or gave you a tough time. Abigail was patient and didn't allow these people to get underneath her skin. God will bless us with the patience to deal with people with different personalities. Many times in ministry or in my business, I deal with lots of people. Some are harder to work with than others. I can recall a time when I had a difficult client. This individual was bossy, prideful, and a pest. I had to pray a lot to deal with her because my spirit would be so grieved after each conversation. Over time, God started to move on this individual and they began to change. I am so glad that I patiently waited on God to handle the situation instead of taking matters into my own hands.

Abigail saved lives. She heard what her husband did, so she had no other choice but to go behind his back and put together a peace offering. Imagine your testimony and prayers saving lives. Someone needs to hear how God set you free. Your story may not be pretty, but it's going to bless someone. You may not feel like you are important because you don't have a title or you operate in the background, but you are. Your prayers are saving lives because they are canceling the plans of the enemy. I bless God for every opportunity to share my testimony because various people have told me how blessed they were. Some were on the verge of committing suicide, giving up, or about to sin, but God used me to be a sound voice in their life. God wants to use you as well.

Abigail had wisdom because she knew what to do when everyone's life was on the line. She brought an abundance of supplies speedily. She wasted no time getting 200 loaves of bread, 5 cooked sheep, a bushel or 32 dry quarts of grain, 100 raisin cakes, and 200 fig cakes (verse 18). She put everything on donkeys and told her servants to go before her. She jumped off her donkey and bowed down before David. God put the right words in her mouth. There were times when God gave me exactly what to do or say in a vision. I acted upon it swiftly and I prospered. As a result, people were blessed. Always pray for wisdom because you will make a difference in someone's life.

Abigail was a quick thinker and that's how we need to be. Every day, we face challenges and have to make decisions. Sometimes, we must decide quickly because some situations are life or death. When I worked as a Respiratory Therapist, in the healthcare field, moments would arise where I had to move swiftly or my patient would die. For instance, I had to put oxygen on a patient who was turning blue. I had to place various breathing machines on them to sustain their lives. In ministry, I had to pray without asking questions when God showed me someone going through a crisis. As a mother, I had to move fast to keep my children safe when they were babies because they would do something dangerous such as trying to go downstairs, touching a hot object, or putting small items into their mouths.

Abigail was discerning because she had a great understanding of various things. She knew how to treat people. We need discernment to know what kind of people we are dealing with. We have to rely on God to be able to discern people's motives. We have to be watchful and be consistent in prayer. Abigail may not have always verbalized how she felt, but she paid attention to her surroundings. We must do the same. Perhaps, you feel like you don't have a voice or you might be discouraged because it seems like your words are falling on deaf ears. However, don't stop being great because the people around you can't see your value. You are God's hidden treasure and you are precious to Him.

Abigail was gorgeous, yet she had more going for herself than just her looks. She was beautiful inside and out. Some women are so superficial. They think that the world revolves around their beauty. Beauty fades over time. When you get older, you might gain weight. Your breasts start to sag. You might get stretch marks from childbirth. Your skin gets wrinkled. Your hair greys. Your posture might not be the best and you now have a hunchback. Some may feel like these characteristics are beautiful but true beauty is in the eyes of the beholder. When I was younger, I was very superficial. I stayed in the mirror for hours, beautifying myself. Since I was a D and F student, I would show my body to draw attention to myself. I did not realize that it was the wrong kind of attention. When I gave my life to Christ, He showed me that I have a brain and how to apply it. I became an honor roll student and started receiving many certificates for making excellent grades. I made the Dean's and President's List multiple times. I graduated with honors and got an Associate's Degree in Respiratory Care. Then I graduated again with honors and obtained my Bachelor's Degree in

Biology and a minor in Chemistry. We have to have more to us than just our looks. We have to have something to fall back on.

Declaration:

I am beautiful and anointed. I am a woman of worth and value. I am a wise woman. I am patient, kind, and discerning. I am loving and quick on my feet.

2

Abishag

Abishag was a beautiful young woman chosen to be King David's concubine when he was old and dying. She cared and served him, but the two never had sex. We can read about her story in 1 Kings 1 and 2 (1 Kings 1:3,15; 2:17, 21-22). Since she was a concubine, her social status was lower than a wife. Some concubines had the same benefits as wives, although not guaranteed. Today we call it shacking. Imagine living with a man who is not your husband. You give him your body and he knows you very intimately. Afterward, he leaves your bed chamber and goes to his wife. You long to spend time with him, but you aren't his priority. You are just an object of pleasure. You bear his children, but they are deemed illegitimate and called "bastards." As a result, they don't have any birthrights or great inheritance since they were conceived with a concubine and not with the wife.

Imagine being a concubine. Some thoughts that could run through your mind are, "Am I not good enough to be your wife?" "Am I just a sex object?" "Am I just a side chick with no benefits?" "I am your second pick and not your first?" "All we do is have sex. I want more from you. Can we go on dates sometimes? Are you too ashamed to be seen with me in public? Can we meet outside of the bedroom sometimes?" Many women are acting like concubines. They settle in life and don't realize their value. They don't mind being a man's side chick and don't care anything about having the benefits of the wife. A wife has the right to property, insurance, and inheritance if the husband was to pass away. It's sad how many women don't get a dime after being with a man for years because they were never married. They did everything a wife does, but there was no true commitment. Their relationship wasn't one of covenant and it wasn't recognized legally. Don't compromise because God has a husband for you.

Abishag was young and her future might have been robbed since she was chosen to be a concubine. Was she attracted to the old King? Imagine having dreams of marrying your prince charming, but that will never happen because you have to be a bedmate. Even though King David was handsome in his youth, looks fade as one ages. Some women may find it appalling to be with an older man. Imagine being looked at only as a sex object. Some people can't look past your beauty. You have a purpose and you are more than a trophy. Many women have been devastated as they aged. Their husbands left them for younger women. They didn't have anything going for themselves because their lives revolved around making their husbands happy. They had no skills or education. Women, we are more than just a pretty object on a man's side. There are so many treasures that the Lord has placed inside of us that we must discover.

The name Abishag means "ignorance of the father or my father strays.[3]" Sometimes, people

3. "H49 - 'Abiyshag - Strong's Hebrew Lexicon (KJV)." Blue Letter Bible. Accessed 18 Oct, 2020. https://www.blueletterbible.org//lang/lexicon/lexicon.cfm?Strongs=H49&t=KJV

can't recognize your worth and deemed you not good enough because of how you look. Imagine a man being so attracted to you that once he has you, he throws you away. He took your most valuable prized possession and defiled it, which is what happened with Tamar and Amnon (2 Samuel 13). He was so mesmerized by his sister's beauty, that he raped her, and then hated her. Abishag could relate. Even though she didn't have sex with the King, she was seen as easy. The King's son Adonijah wanted her to be his wife. It never happened because king Solomon made sure he was executed since he was a threat to the throne. However, if it did, then she would've been tossed from man to man.

There were times where a man was so attracted to me that he couldn't see my worth. I could see his eyes scanning my chest and other areas of my body even though I was dressed modestly. The look of lust penetrated his face but I didn't make a big scene about it. I just pretended that I didn't notice. Some of these men were pastors and when I walked into the room, I could see they were distracted. They kept looking at me from the pulpit or tried to impress me.

Other times, some would invite me to preach just to look at me. They didn't invite me because I could bring the Kingdom of God. Some would message me on social media to get a conversation, but the Lord allowed me to discern their motives, so I didn't entertain them. Some of these men didn't take me seriously. These men couldn't see the anointing. They were caught up in their flesh. I am grateful that God has placed an anointing upon my life. As I minister, they can't refute the hand of the Lord upon me because they see the signs and wonders. As a result, the Lord is glorified.

Many women have wounds that God wants to heal from broken relationships, rejection, and being used and abused. When God heals you, there is a complete work. You will never settle and allow someone to take advantage of you. When a man can't see your worth, they aren't the one. God has a husband for you that will cherish you and he will be able to see past your beauty.

Now that we have summarized Abishag's story, let's look at the following characteristics that she possessed.

- Kind
- Humble
- Strength

She took care of the King when he was dying. She laid with him and kept him warm. When someone is dying, their breathing is labored, phlegm might build up in their throat, and other body fluids might drain. It's not an easy task, so it takes a humble special person to handle it. Men might have said Abishag was insignificant, but God placed these great qualities inside of her to make a difference in David's transition into eternity. The King needed someone kind to care for him as he was in the last stages of his life and Abishag was the right person for the job.

I worked in healthcare for a decade and it was very humbling. People are at their worst, and you have to be strong to handle the challenges as they present themselves. Abishag was able to handle the pain as she witnessed David take his last breath. She was a woman of strength. She had more to her than just her great looks.

Declaration:

I am more than just a sex object and trophy. I am a woman of virtue. I am kind, humble, and strong. I am a woman of great skills and significance.

3

Achsah

ACHSAH WAS DESTINED TO be a wife. Many women are domestic and envision marrying the man of their dreams. She didn't settle for any man, but she waited on God for her husband. We can read about her story in Joshua 15:16-17, Judges 1:12-13. She was wifey material and everyone knew it. There was a time of war, and the Lord commanded Joshua to give Caleb some land. Caleb knew he needed help conquering the land, so he said, "Whoever would attack and conquer the city of Kiriath Sepher, I will give my daughter as your wife." Imagine men being motivated to go to war by the thought of the prize of marrying you. Men will fight for someone virtuous and not someone easy. They want something that not a lot of men have ran through. Why buy the cow when you can get the milk for free? Most men won't marry you when you give them your body. When I was in the world, I was promiscuous and depressed because no man would stay faithful to me. Men love a challenge and Achsah's story is a reminder of how a man will work for you when they know your worth. Jacob worked for many years for Rachel (Genesis 29). Rachel was Jacob's good thing just as Achsah was going to be her husband's good thing (Proverbs 18:22).

Achsah's name means adorned, ankle bracelet, or bursting the veil[4]. The fact that she kept herself pure and waited for marriage before giving away her body made her more beautiful in the men's sight who were going to war. Eventually, Othniel, one of the judges in the Bible, conquered Kiriath Sepher and won Achsah's hand in marriage. Her father, Caleb, gave her husband land as her dowry, but Achsah asked for an addition of springs of water as well.

---

4. "H5915 - `Akcah - Strong's Hebrew Lexicon (KJV)." Blue Letter Bible. Accessed 18 Oct, 2020. https://www.blueletterbible.org//lang/lexicon/lexicon.cfm?Strongs=H5915&t=KJV

Now that we have summarized Achsah's story, let's look at the following characteristics that she possessed.

- Wisdom
- Favor
- Boldness

Achsah had wisdom because she knew that she had favor with her father and needed more than just land. She needed a water supply because her family could trade, survive, have agricultural advancement, wash clothes, and cook. She discerned the right time to ask her father and she received it. Had she waited to ask, then her father might have said no. She was able to discern that her father was in a giving mood. Othniel listened to his wife's counsel. He knew that she was a sound voice and was building up her family with her desire for more. Wisdom will show you how to build. During the 2020 pandemic, God gave me strategies that caused me to prosper and pay off debt, so my family could build wealth and do greater exploits for His Kingdom.

Achsah had favor because her father could've said, "No. The land is enough." However, he honored her request. When you have the favor of God upon your life, people will be kind to you. They will break their own rules to accommodate you. She asked her father for a spring, but he gave her two: the upper and the lower springs (Joshua 15:19). She got a double blessing. The favor of God will attract an overflow to come into your life. Achsah received part of her inheritance, which is amazing because, in her day, women didn't receive anything. They would receive from their husbands when they got married. The favor of God will allow you to get things that you aren't even qualified for. There were times, where God poured so much favor on me that I received things that I didn't ask for. One day, my students from the school of the prophets surprised me with a money cake, gifts, and food. When I went to pull the candle out of the cake, several hundreds of dollars were attached to it. My students went out of their way to bless me. That's God.

Achsah also had boldness. She asked her father for exactly what she desired. She didn't beat around the bush. Some may say that she wasn't satisfied, but there is nothing wrong with wanting more of something in the will of God. She didn't ask for riches, fame, or things that could turn her heart away from God. She asked for a natural resource: water. To reiterate, there is nothing wrong with asking for greater, especially if something is going to cause you and your family to prosper. We serve a big God and He gives us big dreams. That's why when we are in a wilderness season, we yearn for better because we know that God has something better in store for us. Some of us have not because we ask not (James 4:2-3). When my blessing is near, I will be bold and won't stop until I have obtained it.

Declaration:

I am worth marriage and the answer to someone's prayers. I am a beautiful treasure created by the Master's hands. I will be bold and follow the unction of the Holy Spirit. I will receive my inheritance as a daughter of God and will walk in everlasting favor.

4

Bilhah

BILHAH WAS RACHEL'S HANDMAID and a concubine of her husband, Jacob. She had two sons by him, Dan and Naphtali. Bilhah was only a girl when Laban, Rachel's father, assigned her to be her servant. Rachel was about to start a new chapter of her life as Jacob's wife and Bilhah embarked on that journey as well (Genesis 29:29). In Genesis 30:1-7, Bilhah is being used to start a family for Rachel. Rachel is envious of her sister Leah having many children for Jacob. Rachel couldn't have any so she told Jacob to go into Bilhah so she could start a family through her. Imagine being used as a piece of meat or property. While Jacob was being intimate with Bilhah, was he thinking about Rachel the whole time? After the physical act was over, there was no caressing, affection, or being held. Perhaps, he went on with his business or spent time with his wives. Bilhah was strong and a servant. She didn't want to disobey her mistress so she unselfishly gave up her body to make sure Rachel could start a family. She didn't want to fall in love with Jacob and realized that her role was duty over emotion, thus bearing him two sons.

Years later, Reuben, Jacob's oldest son, started sleeping with Bilhah (Genesis 35:22). Was she lonely or longing for the affection of a man? Is this why she slept with Reuben? Perhaps she wanted someone to love her and to have romance. When I was in the world, I slept around because I was lonely and felt empty inside. Jesus Christ eventually filled that void. Bilhah and Reuben's sexual encounter was known all over Israel. Imagine the shame and the embarrassment she faced. People gossiped about what had happened. Her name was probably dragged through the mud. Did Jacob look at her in disgust? He never forgave his son for the shame he put him through (Genesis 49:4). If Bilhah had feelings for Reuben, they could never be a couple publicly because she belonged to his father.

The name Bilhah means bashful or troubled[5]. She was very hidden and overlooked. However, she was significant in the sight of God. Her children are a part of the twelve tribes of Israel (Deuteronomy 27:12-13).

Now that we have summarized her story, let's look at her overriding attribute:

- Servant

She was a servant and gave up her desires for her masters. Every great woman needs to serve in some capacity. Either they are serving their husbands by keeping their house in order or they are serving others with their God-given gifts. Jesus Christ took on the form of a servant even though He was God in the flesh (Philippians 2:7). We can see from their lives to take the lowly route and God will make sure that you are not forgotten. I have dedicated my life to serving

5. "H1090 - Bilhah - Strong's Hebrew Lexicon (KJV)." Blue Letter Bible. Accessed 18 Oct, 2020. https://www.blueletterbible.org//lang/lexicon/lexicon.cfm?Strongs=H1090&t=KJV

others and God has made sure that I am taken care of. He is a true provider and protector.

Declaration:

I am God's servant. I will not get ahead of the Lord but will wait for Him to fulfill His promises in my life. I will delight myself in the Lord, and He will give me the desires of my heart.

5

Dinah

Dinah was the daughter of Leah and Jacob. Her story is told in Genesis 34. She was so very beautiful that Shechem, a Hivite, was attracted to her that he raped her. He was obsessed with her and loved her in his own twisted way (Genesis 34:1-3). Imagine the pain Dinah endured. She lost her virginity in a horrific way. She was robbed of experiencing the first time of intimacy with her future husband because a total stranger defiled her. Shechem overpowered her and she eventually laid there scared and in agony, wishing it would all be over quickly. I can recall when an ex-boyfriend threw my stuff out of a balcony window thirteen stories down. Afterward, he forced himself on me. I gave in because I was afraid that he would kill me if I didn't comply. I cried for two weeks after because I was broken into nothingness. Dinah must've been afraid that she didn't know what else to do. She felt like the scum on the face of the earth and lowered her head in shame. Shechem wouldn't leave her alone. He wanted to marry her. Was Dinah disgusted that she would have to marry her rapist? Could she ever love someone that caused her so much pain? I can understand how broken she felt. Out of fear, I started a relationship with the man who violated me. He was controlling and jealous. He wanted to marry me but I knew that I would've been miserable so instead, I fled. Dinah probably felt trapped and hoped for a way out.

The name Dinah means avenged, vindicated, judgment, and only God will judge.[6] After Shechem defiled her, she stayed at his house. Imagine seeing your rapist daily. His touch would make your skin crawl. His presence would be nauseating. She was crying out for Help. She possessed the following attribute:

- She trusted God for vindication.

---

6. "H1783 - Diynah - Strong's Hebrew Lexicon (KJV)." Blue Letter Bible. Accessed 18 Oct, 2020. https://www.blueletterbible.org//lang/lexicon/lexicon.cfm?Strongs=H1783&t=KJV

After everything she suffered, God is a very present help in the time of trouble. God used Dinah's brothers, Simeon and Levi, to deliver her from a bad situation. They ended up killing Shechem, his father, and other men. Dinah was now free to leave because her violator had received justice for his crime. Jacob was troubled (v. 30) and said to his sons, "You have caused me trouble." They responded (v. 31), "Our sister doesn't deserve to be treated like a prostitute." People may have done you wrong, but God fights for us. He will vindicate you despite the horrific things you have endured. God loves us and will make sure that no one gets away with anything. Will you trust God to right your wrongs? Will you allow Him to fight the battles that you have no control over? Can you pray when it feels like your world is crashing down?

God has vindicated me many times. When I thought it was over for me, He came through. When I cried myself to sleep from the trials that I have suffered, He heard my cry. He humbled my enemies and caused them to apologize to me. I didn't rejoice when they were judged by the hand of the Lord, instead, I prayed for them.

God allowed me to sympathize with them. When someone hurts you, pray, and trust God for vindication. He knows how to judge righteously. God will heal you from trauma and make you whole.

Romans 12:19 says, "Dearly beloved, avenge not yourselves, but rather give place unto wrath: For it is written, Vengeance is mine: I will repay," saith the Lord.

Declaration:

I am loved and protected by God. He will vindicate me and restore me. He will heal me from hurt and make me whole.

6

Elisabeth

ELISABETH WAS THE MOTHER of John the Baptist and the wife of Zechariah. You can read her story in Luke 1. She was an older woman who thought she was too old to become pregnant. However, the Lord blessed her womb and she conceived around the same time as her cousin Mary, who carried Jesus in her womb. The name Elisabeth means God is my oath.[7] An oath is a promise or vow and a great reminder of the faithfulness of the Lord. Let's look at some attributes that she carried:

---

7. "G1665 - elisabet - Strong's Greek Lexicon (KJV)." Blue Letter Bible. Accessed 18 Oct, 2020. https://www.blueletterbible.org//lang/lexicon/lexicon.cfm?Strongs=G1665&t=KJV

- Patience
- Spirit-filled

Elisabeth is the perfect example of being patient and waiting for the promises of the Lord. She may be in Mary's shadows, but she played a key role in the coming of the Lord Jesus Christ. Elisabeth gave birth to a pioneer. Her son John the Baptist was a forerunner for the Messiah. He worked tirelessly in the wilderness baptizing, declaring repentance, and preparing the way for Jesus until decapitated. Elisabeth received a miracle and God will bless us with one as we are patient. Many times we look at the calendar and become weary as the days pass. You aren't forgotten. At the right time, you will receive your promise.

Elisabeth was spirit-filled (Luke 1:41). When Mary, her pregnant cousin, greeted Elisabeth, her baby leaped in her womb and she was filled with the Holy Spirit. Suddenly, she began to prophesy over Mary (v.42-45). When you are full of the Holy Spirit, you will flow and operate in spiritual gifts (1 Corinthians 12:8-10). You may not be pregnant in the natural, but you are in the spirit, and carry something great that will impact nations when birthed.

Declaration:

I am a powerhouse full of the Holy Spirit. I command all the spiritual gifts that are lying dormant within me to be activated and come forth.

7

Eunice and Lois

EUNICE WAS TIMOTHY'S MOTHER (Acts 16:1) and Lois was his grandmother (2 Timothy 1:5). Both of these women were believers in Jesus Christ and their faith was passed down to Timothy. However, Eunice was married to a Greek or an unbeliever. Many women are married to someone that doesn't believe in the Lord. It takes a lot of prayer and faith to believe God for their spouse's salvation. Don't stop believing God for victory. Nothing is too hard for Him. The name Eunice means good victory[8], and Lois means desirable, agreeable, or better[9]. These women were impor-

8. "G2131 - eunikē - Strong's Greek Lexicon (KJV)." Blue Letter Bible. Accessed 18 Oct, 2020. https://www.blueletterbible.org//lang/lexicon/lexicon.cfm?Strongs=G2131&t=KJV
9. "G3090 - lōis - Strong's Greek Lexicon (KJV)." Blue Letter Bible. Accessed 18 Oct, 2020. https://www.blueletterbible.org//lang/lexicon/lexicon.cfm?Strongs=G3090&t=KJV

tant in God's sight. They were gatekeepers of their home. Let's look at the following attribute they both possessed:

- Faith

These women did their best to be a positive role model for Timothy. They probably were full of the Spirit of God and prayer warriors. Perhaps they gathered with other believers and took Timothy along so they all could hear the gospel preached. Maybe they lived a supernatural life and demonstrated the power of God. Whatever these women did, Timothy's life was greatly impacted. He was able to co-labor in the gospel with Apostle Paul. These women trained Timothy in the fear and admonition of the Lord. You may not feel like you are making a difference, but your children or grandchildren will come back to their roots or the foundation of what you taught them. They will remember the prayers you prayed. They watch how you live. Every time you pick up your Bible to read it, they take notice. The world needs more godly women imparting into the next generation. Are you up for the task?

Proverbs 22:6 says, "Train up a child in the way he should go: and when he is old, he will not depart from it."

Declaration:

I will be a positive role model for my family. I will share the Word of God and pray with my family. I will raise my children and grand-children in the ways of the Lord.

8

Euodia and Syntyche

Euodia and Syntyche were powerful women of God in the Philippian church. However, they were blind sighted by division and had a public disagreement. Everybody knew that these women didn't get along, so Apostle Paul wrote a letter for them to make peace. He had worked with both of them and knew that the enemy was in operation behind the scenes. Their story is told in Philippians 4:2-3. The name Euodia means sweet fragrance[10] and Syntyche means fortune

---

10. "G2136 - euodia - Strong's Greek Lexicon (KJV)." Blue Letter Bible. Accessed 18 Oct, 2020. https://www.blueletterbible.org//lang/lexicon/lexicon.cfm?Strongs=G2136&t=KJV

or fate[11]. As we delve into their lives, we can see how they had to learn conflict management.

James 3:16 says, "For where envying and strife is, there is confusion and every evil work."

- Conflict management

Were these women in competition with each other? Many can't focus on their own God-given assignment because they are so busy trying to outdo someone else. Was jealousy in operation? Jealousy happens when you don't know who you are in God and feel threatened by someone else. Your assignment may be different from the other person, so why hate? We all have work to do and need each other (1 Corinthians 12:12-27).

People will often get upset with me because they don't like the message I preached or a status I wrote on social media. Perhaps they got offended when I rebuked them if they were in my mentoring network. Some of these individu-

11. "G4941 - syntychē - Strong's Greek Lexicon (KJV)." Blue Letter Bible. Accessed 18 Oct, 2020. https://www.blueletterbible.org//lang/lexicon/lexicon.cfm?Strongs=G4941&t=KJV

als went to their social media accounts or went behind my back to sow discord. I made sure to keep the matter private and handle conflict in a biblical way (Matthew 18:15-17). Even though they attacked me publicly, I held my peace and prayed. God vindicated me each time.

We are called to be peacemakers (Romans 12:18). We must forgive and pray for one another. I discovered that I won't easily take offense or become jealous of someone that I am constantly praying over. Are you praying for the person that you may be at odds with? People are watching us and how we respond. Do your actions glorify God or the devil?

Euodia and Syntyche failed momentarily to keep the overall vision in focus. They didn't appreciate each other's gifts or the qualities they possessed. God will allow us to work with different people to help us grow and for His will to be accomplished. People may not see what you see, flow like you, or preach like you. However, they are important to God because they are His handiwork. Let things go. Love people while they are here because people die daily. You don't want that blood on your hands.

Declaration:

I will walk in love and pray for those that I disagree with. I will handle conflict in a biblical manner and will not cause a public scandal. I will be a peacemaker.

9

Hagar

THE STORY OF HAGAR involves pride, reaping, and mercy. We can read her story in Genesis 16 and 21. Her name means a stranger, one that fears, forsaken, flight, and a famous bearer.[12] Her life matches these different meanings of her because of what she endured. Hagar was the slave girl to Sarah, Abraham's wife. Also, Hagar is the mother of Ismael, the son she had with Abraham. Sarah was old and couldn't have any children of her own. She had a promise from the Lord that one day she would have a child but she grew impatient. As a result, she offered Hagar to her husband to start a family through her.

12. "H1904 - Hagar - Strong's Hebrew Lexicon (KJV)." Blue Letter Bible. Accessed 18 Oct, 2020. https://www.blueletterbible.org//lang/lexicon/lexicon.cfm?Strongs=H1904&t=KJV

Things didn't work out and later, Hagar and Ismael were sent away. It was never Hagar's plan to sleep with Abraham. Have you ever been used before? Hagar can relate because after her mistress didn't find her useful anymore, she kicked her to the curb. She had nowhere to go and thought she and her son would die out in the hot desert. The desert is a dry place and water is hard to find. It gets extremely cold at night, and there are many creatures such as scorpions, foxes, spiders, snakes, and vultures that are looking for prey. Once Sarah had her own promise child, she forfeited the original plan of Hagar starting a family for her. Let's look at an attribute Hagar possessed:

- Repentant heart

Psalms 51:17 (GNT) says, "My sacrifice is a humble spirit, O God; you will not reject a humble and repentant heart."

Once Hagar became pregnant, she started to change and become prideful. Hagar couldn't handle the blessing of conception properly. She started to feel like she was better than Sarah and forgot that she was just a slave. Her job was to serve Sarah and the child she carried was supposed to help her mistress start a family of her own, which was a common practice in that era. Sometimes when you get blessed, you forget who you are or lose focus of the vision. Hagar started mistreating and despised Sarah. As a result, Sarah became harsh with her and Hagar fled into the desert. Hagar had reaped what she had sown.

Galatians 6:7 (ESV) says, "Do not be deceived: God is not mocked, for whatever one sows, that will he also reap."

After Hagar fled, she repented to God and He extended His mercy. The Lord sent her a message through an angel. The child that she carried would one day become a great nation. The angel instructed her to return to her mistress and she obeyed. Years later, Ismael was making fun of Isaac (the promised child). Sarah got upset and sent Hagar and Ishmael away. Maybe Sarah was threatened by her and when the first opportunity arose for her to be terminated from the position, she acted upon it. Kids will be kids and most of them aren't mature. They don't think about the consequences of their actions, so they say and do hurtful things. Instead of giving Hagar and her son a rebuke so they can learn what not to do, she just kicked them to the curb. Hagar was disregarded once again but God took care of her and son. They could've died in the wilderness but she knew how to get a hold of the Lord.

The Lord sent another angel. Most people never had an angelic visitation but she was blessed to experience two encounters. She experienced the supernatural. The angel made water appear in the desert so they wouldn't die. The human body needs water to survive. God made sure that Hagar and her son weren't left out of the promise. Hagar is also the mother of nations. Even though she is in Sarah's shadow, God still blessed her and took care of her and her descendants. Maybe her mistress ended up jealous of her and had difficulty seeing her advance, and be happy. As you continue to walk uprightly before the Lord, He will bless you and extend His goodness in your life.

Declaration:

I am special to God regardless of how anyone feels. The Lord loves my family and me. I will experience the Lord's provision for my life. I will be quick to repent.

10

Jael

JAEL WAS THE CHOSEN woman who killed the evil commander Sisera so the Israelites could be free from King Jabin. Her story is read in Judges 4 and 5. Jael was married to Heber, the Kenite. Her name means mountain goat.[13] Once prophetess Deborah prophesied that the Israelites were going to be set free, Jael responded to that word. Now that we have summarized her story, let's review the following attribute concerning Jael:

- Brave

13. "H3278 - Ya`el - Strong's Hebrew Lexicon (KJV)." Blue Letter Bible. Accessed 18 Oct, 2020. https://www.blueletterbible.org//lang/lexicon/lexicon.cfm?Strongs=H3278&t=KJV

In Judges 4 and 5, it was looked down upon for a woman to get the credit over a man. However, it was the Lord's choice. He wanted to use that woman who was overlooked so He would get the glory. Deborah prophesied that Barak would not get credit but a woman (Judges 4:9). Sisera oppressed the Israelites for twenty years and they cried out to the Lord for help. During the day of battle, the Lord confused Sisera's army and chariots. All of his men were killed, so Sisera fled the chariot and ran away on foot. He came upon Jael's tent because he was tired and thirsty and needed rest. She invited him in and gave him some milk. He drank it and she covered him with a mantle. He fell asleep and Jael took a nail and hammered it into his skull. Sisera died instantly. It took courageousness to face your enemy and not shrink back.

God will use His daughters to tread new territory for His glory and anoint them to soar above the adversity. He will give His women servants wisdom to lead so they can be quick on their feet. God is equipping them for battle. We must go deeper into prayer so we can be sensitive to the Spirit of God. Jael was able to fulfill the prophecy and we must take the prophetic words spoken over us and war with them. We are immovable and unshakeable in Jesus Christ. Nothing can stop what God wants to do in our lives.

Declaration:

I am a demon slayer and will set my face like a flint. I won't be intimidated by warfare but lean on God to strengthen me so I can push past it.

11

Jehosheba

JEHOSHEBA'S STORY CAN BE read in 2 Kings 11. Her name means Yahweh is an oath or Jehovah is sworn.[14] She was the wife of Jehoiada, the priest and the daughter of Jehoram. Jehoram's son was Ahaziah, but Jehu killed him along with all his brothers and nephews (2 Kings 9). However, Ahaziah just had a baby named Joash and Jehosheba hid him for six years in the temple. Her husband, Jehoiada, commanded a group of men to guard the young King with their lives. Joash is in Jesus' Christ lineage, and the enemy almost destroyed it because the evil Athaliah (Jezebel's daughter) had killed all the royal heirs

14. "H3089 - Yehowsheba` - Strong's Hebrew Lexicon (KJV)." Blue Letter Bible. Accessed 18 Oct, 2020. https://www.blueletterbible.org//lang/lexicon/lexicon.cfm?Strongs=H3089&t=KJV

and claimed the throne. She was queen for about six years until one day, Jehoiada and his men crowned Joash King. Then they killed the wicked queen. Now that we have summarized Jehosheba's story, let's look at her characteristic:

- Risk Taker

Jehosheba was a risk-taker and she put her life on the line. She was related to Athaliah because she could've been her biological daughter or stepdaughter. Athaliah was married to her father, Jehoram. Jehosheba recognized the wickedness and knew that Athaliah had no legal claim to the throne, so she saved her nephew, who was the legitimate heir. If Athaliah would've found out what Jehosheba had done, she would've been killed just like everyone else in the royal family. Maybe Athaliah didn't see Jehosheba as a threat and overlooked her. God loves to use those people that have been overlooked and counted out. People might have dismissed you because of your beauty, position, and lack of connections. However, for those reasons, God will pour out His Spirit on you for a divine assignment.

We have to realize that our assignments from God are bigger than us. The enemy will try everything to sabotage it, just like he did in 2 Kings 11. The devil strategically attacked the Davidic lineage because he knew that Jesus would come through that bloodline. Count it not strange when you are doing the right thing and you come underneath warfare. You are anointed to handle it and God will even cause you to be stealthy like he did with Jehosheba. The enemy had no idea what she had done. God will use you as His weapon of war and allow you to tear down the kingdom of darkness as you become a risk-taker.

Declaration:

I am bold, courageous, and Spirit-filled. I am more than a conqueror in Jesus' Christ. I am untraceable in the realm of the spirit, so the enemy doesn't know what I am doing for the Lord.

12

Joanna

JOANNA WAS THE WIFE of Cuza and a financial supporter of Jesus' ministry (Luke 8:3). Her name means God is gracious.[15] She was also one of the women who went to prepare Jesus' body for burial. They had spices prepared for his body (Luke 24:10), but they saw the stone rolled back from the tomb and saw two angels. The angels told these women that Jesus had risen. Joanna and the other went to tell the Apostles, but they refused to listen. Let's look at two of her attributes:

---

15. "G2490 - iōanan - Strong's Greek Lexicon (KJV)." Blue Letter Bible. Accessed 18 Oct, 2020. https://www.blueletterbible.org//lang/lexicon/lexicon.cfm?Strongs=G2490&t=KJV

- Caretaker
- Financial supporter

Joanne had to be strong because not everyone can handle seeing the Lord in that way. He was beaten beyond recognition (Isiah 52:14), but she was prepared to clean up the wounds, wrapped his bloody body, and anoint him for burial. She was doing her ministry, cleaning up, and making something (his house) look better. Many people don't want to clean up the Lord's house (church building) because it's not glamorous or one of notoriety. However, we need a clean place to worship. God usually raises up the lowly and sends them from the back to the forefront. She was blessed to have a supernatural encounter with these angelic beings.

Joanne was a financial supporter of Jesus Christ. In ministry, it takes money and resources to do what you are called to do. You can do more things for God and others when you have finances. How can you effectively help someone pay their bills when your lights are about to get cut off, you need gas in your car, and you barely have any food in your home? When you give financially and support a ministry, you are partnering with the man or woman of God spiritually. Whatever blessings or harvest they partake of, so will you. Your reward will be great for being an underwriter because God used your resources to make it possible. For instance, the church's rent, the utilities, and the advertising bills were paid. The ministry had more outreach resources because of your unselfishness. You trusted God to put money in your hands because you know He gives seed to the sower. You know that you will get the funds right back because when you give, it will be given unto you (Luke 6:38).

Declaration:

I am selfless, kind, compassionate, and will esteem others above myself. I will love my neighbors as myself. I trust God more than I trust money.

13

Jochebed

JOCHEBED WAS THE MOTHER of Moses, Aaron, and Miriam. Her name means God's glory[16] and she was married to Amram (Exodus 6:20; Numbers 26:59). We can read about her story in Exodus and Numbers. She birthed three prophets and most likely, she was prophetic herself. Let's look at some characteristics she possessed:

- Justice
- Favor

When Moses was born, the wicked Pharaoh was threatened by the Hebrews and wanted

16. "H3115 - Yowkebed - Strong's Hebrew Lexicon (KJV)." Blue Letter Bible. Accessed 18 Oct, 2020. https://www.blueletterbible.org//lang/lexicon/lexicon.cfm?Strongs=H3115&t=KJV

to commit genocide. He ordered all the males born to be thrown into the Nile River or killed (Exodus 1:16, 22). Jochebed knew that this was demonic and not right in the sight of God, so she stood for justice. She didn't follow the evil decree of killing her son. Instead, she chose to hide her son for three months until she couldn't any longer. One day she decided to put in him a basket on the Nile River. She prayed for his protection, and she assigned her daughter Miriam to watch him from afar (Exodus 2).

We can learn from Jochebed that as believers in Jesus Christ that we don't have to obey laws that are contrary to our faith. The world will call us rebellious, but it's better to please God and obey Him than man (Acts 5:29). We can refuse to comply. For instance, King Nebuchadnezzar ordered everyone to bow down to his statute and three Hebrew men refused (Daniel 3) because they knew the Lord's commands of not serving any other gods (Exodus 20:3). Jochebed knew that God commanded His people not to kill (Exodus 20:13) and killing innocent babies is a form of abortion or infanticide. Jochebed trusted God with her son, and God used all her children to do great exploits for Him.

Jochebed had God's favor because after she put Moses in a basket in the Nile River, the Pharaoh's daughter found him. The Pharaoh's daughter decided to spare the child and raise him like her own son. She could provide a good life of having the best of everything because of her socioeconomic status. When she laid eyes upon baby Moses, Miriam approached her and told her that she could help find a woman to nurse the child. Amazingly, Jochebed was blessed to raise her own son and nurse him until he was weaned. God spared Jochebed the heartache of losing her son. Afterward, she sent him to go live with the Pharaoh's daughter. Jochebed's sacrifice was honored because God allowed her to still be connected to her child.

When God favors you, He will amaze you and blow your mind. Even when Moses aged, he was closed with his siblings, Aaron and Miriam. You may feel insignificant because you feel like you are just a mom and nothing else. That is far from the truth. You are very significant like Jochebed because God is trusting you to care for the next generation of leaders. Your child will thank and honor you as they become older for your love and sacrifice.

Declaration:

My children and grandchildren will do great exploits for the Lord. I will stand up for righteousness and bear the light of Jesus' Christ. I will stand against evil and pray for the Kingdom of Heaven to come down to earth.

14

Junia

ROMANS 16:7 (NKJV) SAYS, *"Greet Andronicus and Junia, my countrymen and my fellow prisoners, who are of note among the apostles, who also were in Christ before me."*

Junia was a female apostle mentioned in Romans 16:7. Her name means youthful[17]17. Many people don't believe in female apostles, but there is no gender in the spirit.

Galatians 3:28 (ESV) says, "There is neither Jew nor Greek, there is neither slave nor free, there

17. "G2458 - iounias - Strong's Greek Lexicon (KJV)." Blue Letter Bible. Accessed 18 Oct, 2020. https://www.blueletterbible.org//lang/lexicon/lexicon.cfm?Strongs=G2458&t=KJV

is no male and female, for you are all one in Christ Jesus.

If there is no one to fill a position, then God will use who is available. Many women have faced persecution in ministry that are in the office of an apostle. God chose them to complete certain mandates and anointed them with a greater level of power (Luke 9:1). Let's look at one of Junia's attributes:

- Endurance

Junia was with Apostle Paul in prison. She had to endure many hardships and keep the vision of the Lord Jesus Christ before her. She knew that assignment was heavy and many souls needed to hear the Gospel . God used her to encourage Apostle Paul and possibly give him advice along his journey because she was a believer way before him. Junia was known in her community and God made sure that signs and wonders followed her. She didn't just come with a title, but she came with demonstration.

1 Corinthians 4:20 says, "For the kingdom of God is not in word, but in power."

When the people saw the way the Lord used her, no one could refute that she was an apostle. Junia teaches us to just do the work and not get caught up in titles. Since she had done many works in her circle, God made sure that her name was great. If you are attacked because you are in a certain office, don't worry. Those people are ignorant of Scripture and need to be educated. Pray that they receive a revelation and keep it moving. The enemy is using your persecutors to distract you. Junia was in prison, still doing the Lord's work. What's your excuse?

Declaration:

I will endure hardships as a good soldier in the Lord Jesus Christ. I will complete my assignment on this earth and will not allow distractions to hinder me.

15

Keturah

Keturah was the second wife of Abraham (Genesis 25:1). After Sarah died, Abraham married his concubine, Keturah and they had sons: Ephah, Epher, Hanoch, Abida, and Eldaah (Genesis 25:4). Keturah's name means incense[18]. She provided a great fragrance symbolically that was appealing to her husband's senses. For instance, many people burn incense to feel better or to make their homes smell nice. That's what Keturah represented to Abraham. His world was shattered after Sarah's passing. After he finished grieving her, he remarried. He chose Keturah

18. "H6989 - Qetuwrah - Strong's Hebrew Lexicon (KJV)." Blue Letter Bible. Accessed 18 Oct, 2020. https://www.blueletterbible.org//lang/lexicon/lexicon.cfm?Strongs=H6989&t=KJV

because she brightened and refreshed his day. Let's look at an attribute that she carried:

- Confident

Keturah was in Sarah's shadows, but she had confidence. It takes a strong woman to not be intimidated by the first wife's legacy. You are called to minister to your husband and your love will keep him alive longer. Most people die soon after losing a spouse due to heartache. Keturah is a great example of the Lord's restoration. God is so gracious that He doesn't allow us to stay in something forever. Weeping may endure for a night, but joy comes in the morning (Psalm 30:5). Keturah encouraged Abraham to continue on his journey and was a companion. It got lonely after his 1st wife died. Now, he had another reason to smile because Keturah brought peace to him. She was a good wife and his crown.

Proverbs 12:4 (NKJV) says, "An excellent wife is the crown of her husband, but she who causes shame is like rottenness in his bones."

If you are married to someone who has been married before or widowed, don't try to be like the first wife, be yourself. You have a different personality and that makes you unique. Because you love your husband, you care about what he cherished. Respect him and know that he holds a special place for you in his heart that no one can replace. Keturah partook of the blessing of Abraham. She had many sons and their names were recorded. God will make sure that your history isn't lost. She was a concubine but God elevated her to become a wife. Don't despise small beginnings. You may be at the bottom, but God will raise you up for His glory.

Declaration:

I am my husband's crown. I bring him peace, comfort, and companionship. I will not be intimidated by any woman because I am confident about my position in his life.

16

Lydia

ACTS 16:14-15 (NKJV) SAYS, *"Now a certain woman named Lydia heard us. She was a seller of purple from the city of Thyatira, who worshipped God. The Lord opened her heart to heed the things spoken by Paul. 15 And when she and her household were baptized, she begged us, saying, "If you have judged me to be faithful to the Lord, come to my house and stay." So she persuaded us."*

Lydia means beautiful, strife, or noble one.[19] She was a successful businesswoman mentioned in Acts 16:14-15 and worshipper. God opened

19. "H3865 - Luwd - Strong's Hebrew Lexicon (KJV)." Blue Letter Bible. Accessed 18 Oct, 2020. https://www.blueletterbible.org//lang/lexicon/lexicon.cfm?Strongs=H3865&t=KJV

up her heart to hear the gospel. Let's look at some of her characteristics:

- Business mogul
- Worshipper
- Yielded

Lydia had great taste and was a business mogul. She set a high standard for others and helped care for her family. She sold expensive purple fabric. Purple stands for royalty, which represents the children of God. She knew that she had to produce quality products unto the Lord. We must ensure that everything we are doing for God is top-notch: books, podcasts, movies, plays, blogs, vlogs, business, etc. People will know that we walk in a spirit of excellence and everything that we do is extraordinary. God will cause you to succeed and bless the work of your hands.

Isaiah 48:17 says, "I am the Lord your God, who teaches you to profit, who leads you in the way you should go."

Lydia enjoyed ministering to the Lord with her worship. She sang from the depths of her soul, beautiful hymns, and songs. She knew that worship ushered in the Lord's presence and was addicted. She longed to spend time with Him because He would download ideas and strategies to advance in life. She loved to feel His fire on her skin and hearing His voice. God is calling us into deeper realms of worship. A few years ago, the Lord told me that worship brings in the harvest. I learned to get in His presence, so He will provide all my needs.

Lydia yielded her heart unto God. Since she had a relationship with Him, her spirit was quickened by the words that Apostle Paul spoke. Instantly, she knew that he knew the Lord in a way that she didn't. She needed to go to another level in God and that involved being baptized, which was one of the things Apostle Paul taught. Lydia humbled herself and paid attention to the gospel because her life would never be the same. As a result, Lydia and her household were baptized. She was so grateful that she wanted to bless Paul and his men by inviting them to stay in her home. She knew that if she blessed him, then God would bless her. Also, she knew that if an apostle of the Lord stayed in her home, her household would be blessed. God will reward your sacrifices of blessing His servants. Your obedience to Him is not in vain.

Declaration:

I will succeed in every area of my life. I will yield myself to the Lord so I can be in sync with His Spirit. I will remain teachable, so I can always go to the next level in God.

17

Persis, Tryphena, and Tryphosa

ROMANS 16:12 (EXB) SAYS, *"Greetings to Tryphena and Tryphosa, ·women who work very hard for [L laborers in] the Lord. Greetings to ·my dear friend [the beloved] Persis, who also has worked very hard ·for [L in] the Lord."*

Persis' name means Persian woman in Greek[20]. She was a great friend of Apostle Paul and she worked very hard in the Lord. Try-

20. "G4069 - persis - Strong's Greek Lexicon (KJV)." Blue Letter Bible. Accessed 18 Oct, 2020. https://www.blueletterbible.org//lang/lexicon/lexicon.cfm?Strongs=G4069&t=KJV

phena's and Tryphosa's names mean delicate or luxurious[21]. Both women had the following characteristic:

- Hard worker

Ministry is more than just having a microphone and preaching behind a pulpit. It's never-ending because there is so much to be done behind the scenes. You may start off small, but the Lord will expand your territory over time and you will need help. People always need prayer and they will contact you all times of the day even if you are exhausted and finished ministering, someone requires your service. People are hungry and lack resources. They need the help that the ministry can offer them. Some are about to backslide, commit suicide, become broken, and lost.

Ministers have to hear the Lord and be led by Him so that He can order their steps. God gives His servants projects to work on so the gospel can be spread further. Books, articles,

---

21. "G5170 - tryphaina - Strong's Greek Lexicon (KJV)." Blue Letter Bible. Accessed 18 Oct, 2020. https://www.blueletterbible.org//lang/lexicon/lexicon.cfm?Strongs=G5170&t=KJV

pamphlets, tracks, and Bibles must be written, printed, and distributed. There is an administrative side of ministry. Events must be planned, funded, and organized. Taxes, licenses, bookkeeping, paperwork, and employees are things that must be handled. The minister must have time to pray and study the Bible to bring Rhema from heaven regularly.

The ant is considered as hardworking. They don't have anyone breathing down their backs, controlling their every move. They have their vision ahead of them and must complete their goals.

Proverbs 6:6-8 (NKJV) says, "Go to the ant, you sluggard! Consider her ways and be wise,
7 Which, having no [d]captain, Overseer or ruler, 8 Provides her [e]supplies in the summer,
And gathers her food in the harvest."

Persis, Tryphena, and Tryphosa, kept the Lord Jesus before them as they spent long hours doing what was required. These women worked late into the night and arose early in the morning. While everyone else was partying or playing around, they were about the Father's business. They had fruit from their labor and their reward was great in heaven. The hands of the diligence make you rich (Proverbs 13:4). As you commit your work unto the Lord, your plans will be established (Proverbs 16:3). People may not know your name, but you are significant in the Lord's sight if you are a laborer in the gospel.

Matthew 9:37-38 (NKJV) says, "Then He said to His disciples, "The harvest truly is plentiful, but the laborers are few. Therefore pray to the Lord of the harvest to send out laborers into His harvest."

Declaration:

I am a laborer of the gospel of Jesus Christ and a soul winner. I will work hard because my reward will be great. I will allow nothing to get in the way of my God-given assignment.

18

Phoebe

ROMANS 16:1 (NKJV) SAYS, "*I commend to you Phoebe our sister, who is a servant of the church in Cenchrea,*"

Phoebe is mentioned in Romans 16:1 and highly recommended by Apostle Paul. She was a deaconess of the Cenchrean church. Her name means bright, radiant, and shining.[22] Let's look at a characteristic that she possessed:

- Deacon

22. "G5402 - phoibē - Strong's Greek Lexicon (KJV)." Blue Letter Bible. Accessed 18 Oct, 2020. https://www.blueletterbible.org//lang/lexicon/lexicon.cfm?Strongs=G5402&t=KJV

Being a deacon is no small task. You are called to take the load off the pastor or the leader that you are serving. You might find yourself preaching when the leader is away at another engagement. You will be required to do outreach ministry while the pastor is serving elsewhere or alongside you in the community. Wherever a need arises, you must be willing to serve. Phoebe was a great support to the church because she kept things running smoothly. Whenever someone needed prayer, she stepped up. If there was a meeting, she rolled up her sleeves, working hard to ensure that the Holy Spirit could do what He wanted and that the people got what they needed. Phoebe assisted the leadership at the church so they wouldn't be overwhelmed. Phoebe was a holy woman and had all the qualifications listed in 1 Timothy 3:8–13.

- Respected (v. 8)
- Kind {Not deceitful} (v.8)
- Doesn't drink too much wine (v.8)
- Not greedy (v.8)
- Keep the faith (v.9)
- Blameless (v.10)
- Self-controlled (v.11)

- Trustworthy (v.11)
- Non-gossipper (v.11)
- Be the husband of one wife (v. 12)
- Be the wife of one husband (v.12)
- Rule their households well (v.12)
- Boldness (v.13)

Phoebe's story teaches us that being a deaconess is a huge task.

Luke 12:48 says, "For unto whomsoever much is given, of him shall be much required."

You are a leader and important in God's sight. You are lifting up your leader's arms and they need you as a crutch for their journey. Stay submitted and know your place in the body of Christ. You might not be called to the five-fold office (Ephesians 4:8-11) or have a title in front of your name. However, your reward will be great because of your service in the Lord's church.

Declaration:

I am a servant, bold, faithful, trustworthy, self-controlled, blameless, kind, respected, not greedy, non-gossiper, and only have one spouse in Jesus' name.

19

Priscilla

PRISCILLA'S NAME MEANS ANCIENT.[23] She was married to Aquila. Together, she and her husband co-labored with Apostle Paul in ministry (Acts 18:2, 18, 26; Rom. 16:3–4; 1 Cor. 16:19). There are different ministries and they function differently. Some have the husband more prominent and the wife in the background. Others have the wife in the forefront and the husband as the supporter. Priscilla and her husband, Aquila, were a team. Let's look at some of their characteristics:

- Husband and wife team

23. "G4252 - priskilla - Strong's Greek Lexicon (KJV)." Blue Letter Bible. Accessed 18 Oct, 2020. https://www.blueletterbible.org//lang/lexicon/lexicon.cfm?Strongs=G4252&t=KJV

- Mentors

There are horror stories of men stopping their wives from preaching and fulfilling her calling in the Lord. Likewise, some women become jealous of their husbands and become a heartache instead of a helpmate. When things are peaceful in your home, then ministry becomes easier to do. If you are stressed out at home, then you will be less effective in your assignment. Priscilla knew her role. She recognized that she was better at some things and her husband vice versa. She never competed with Aquila. If the Holy Spirit was on her husband, she would yield and allow the Lord to use her spouse. When her husband had a word, she supported him. Priscilla and her husband learned how to flow together. Afterward, they prayed for one another. If one lacked something, the other would go the extra mile to make something possible.

Ecclesiastes 4:9-12 says, "9 Two are better than one; because they have a good reward for their labour. 10 For if they fall, the one will lift up his fellow: but woe to him that is alone when he falleth; for he hath not another to help him up. 11 Again, if two lie together, then they have heat: but how can one be warm alone? [12] And if one prevail against him, two shall withstand him; and a threefold cord is not quickly broken."

Priscilla and Aquilla had wisdom and they were great mentors and spiritual parents. They were at the synagogue one day and heard a young man named Apollos speaking boldly. They noticed that he wasn't quite knowledgeable of the gospel, so they took him to their home and explained the ways of God more precisely so he could better understand (Acts 18:26). After they finished mentoring Apollos, he went to another level in his ministry. Apollos was able to prove with Scriptures that Jesus was the Messiah. If you are a mentor, you are appreciated and needed. Someone is praying for you to come into their life.

Declaration:

I will be confident in who I am. I will not be intimidated by another's success. I will support and celebrate others.

20

Puah and Shiphrah

PUAH MEANS LASS, SPLENDID, or little girl.[24] Shiphrah means beautiful or to be fair.[25] Their story begins in Exodus 1:15-21. These are two Hebrew midwives who were ordered by Pharaoh to kill Hebrew babies. They told the Pharaoh that the Hebrew women were different and stronger from the Egyptian women and had their babies on their own before they could get there. They feared the Lord and refused to do what the Pha-

24. “H6326 - Puw`ah - Strong’s Hebrew Lexicon (KJV).” Blue Letter Bible. Accessed 18 Oct, 2020. https://www.blueletterbible.org//lang/lexicon/lexicon.cfm?Strongs=H6326&t=KJV

25 . ”H8236 - Shiphrah - Strong’s Hebrew Lexicon (KJV).” Blue Letter Bible. Accessed 18 Oct, 2020. https://www.blueletterbible.org//lang/lexicon/lexicon.cfm?Strongs=H8236&t=KJV

raoh asked. The Lord blessed these two women mightily and the Hebrew people continued to grow stronger. They had the following attribute:

- Reverence for the Lord

Since these women feared the Lord, they experienced His goodness. There is a great correlation between the fear of the Lord and His blessings.

Psalms 31:19 (NASB) says, "How great is Your goodness, Which You have stored up for those who fear You."

Psalm 112:1(NASB) says, "Praise the Lord! How blessed is the man who fears the Lord, Who greatly delights in His commandments."

Psalm 115:13 (NASB) says, "He will bless those who fear the Lord, The small together with the great."

Puah and Shiphrah knew that if they followed the Pharaoh's orders, they would be sinning against God. We can learn from their stories that if we do what is right in the Lord's sight, we will be blessed in the end. The weapons may form against us, but the Lord will not allow them to prosper. Nothing the enemy says or does can hurt us in any way. Many healthcare workers' faith has been tested. Some were asked to do things contrary to the Word of God. Some were fired for their refusal and the Lord blessed them with double for their trouble. In the natural, it may look like you are losing when you face challenges. However, nothing is too hard for God and He will protect and make a way for you.

Declaration:

I will be bold and not fear. I will trust God for His protection and provision. I am a woman of character and worth.

Sheerah

SHEERAH'S NAME MEANS LIGHT or kinswoman[26]. She was Ephraim's daughter and built three towns.

1 Chronicles 7:24 says, "Ephraim's daughter was Sheerah. She built Lower Beth Horon, Upper Beth Horon, and Uzzen Sheerah."

Let's look at some of her characteristics:

- Good decision making
- Great management

---

26. "H7609 - She'erah - Strong's Hebrew Lexicon (KJV)." Blue Letter Bible. Accessed 18 Oct, 2020. https://www.blueletterbible.org//lang/lexicon/lexicon.cfm?Strongs=H7609&t=KJV

Sheerah had great decision-making skills because she had to determine where she was going to build her towns. Was the land profitable? What kind of people reside there? Is there a water supply? Will there be any attractions to attract tourists? Will the towns have a supply of money? Who will help you run your city? What jobs are available? What is the best mode of transportation in your city? How will your town be able to connect with the next town? Perhaps these were some of the questions that Sheerah had to answer. Many are praying for a house, but maybe God wants to give you a town as He did for Sheerah. We have to think bigger because we serve a big God.

She had great management skills because after the first two towns were built, she started the third one. Sheerah is a great example of a kingdom builder. She started from rock bottom and God added increase. She was able to provide a place for people to live and to be around other believers. She was a businesswoman and had real estate. God will bless His people to own land and property to build churches, schools, organizations, farms, and businesses. They will even create jobs for secular people, so they will know that a Christian is in charge and that God is the source of the blessing. God's people will have assets, so no one can fire them or stop them from doing their assignments. Sheerah is another example of wealth transfer. God used the least likely person, a woman, to build towns. God will shift your life where you go from renting to owning. You will go from working for someone to creating jobs for others. Be open to what God wants to do in your life.

Declaration:

I will lend to many nations and not borrow. I will walk in abundance and experience the goodness of the Lord.

22

Tabitha

Tabitha is also called Dorcas in Greek. Both names mean gazelle[27], which are graceful and swift animals. Her story begins in Acts 9:36-42. She was a charitable woman and made clothing. She had gotten sick and died. Two messengers begged Apostle Peter to come to her house. When he arrived, a crowd of people were outside of the window crying. He sent everyone out of the room, kneeled, and prayed. Then he commanded her to arise. She opened her eyes and sat up. When people heard about what happened to Tabitha, they believed in Jesus Christ. Let's look at some of Tabitha's attributes:

27. "G5000 - tabitha - Strong's Greek Lexicon (KJV)." Blue Letter Bible. Accessed 18 Oct, 2020. https://www.blueletterbible.org//lang/lexicon/lexicon.cfm?Strongs=G5000&t=KJV

- Giver
- Give alms
- Experienced the miraculous
- Creativity

Tabitha performed good deeds and was a giving woman. God used her to finance His Kingdom. Many people may feel like you aren't important unless you have the microphone preaching. However, that's far from the truth. We all have a role to play. Giving is a gift (Romans 12:8). God has raised up people to have wealth to fund various needs in the body of Christ. Running a ministry isn't free. The costs involve hiring staff, website maintenance, advertising, equipment, rent, utilities, outreaching, and more. The more money involved, the greater the reach and spread of the gospel of Jesus Christ. If God has given you the gift of giving, you are making a tremendous difference. God trusts you with money because He knows you are a good steward over it and you won't turn your back on Him. Just be led to the ministry you are supposed to underwrite. Tabitha was a very important woman in her community, that's why many people were in her room and outside her window mourning when she died.

Tabitha gave alms or took care of the poor and needy. God gave her compassion for the less fortunate such as widows, orphans, the homeless, and the poor. Since she had wealth, she was in a position to give unto them. She truly had the heart of God and the Lord favored her even more. When she gave unto the poor, she was lending to the Lord (Proverbs 19:17). When a need arose, the Lord provided. Your outreach ministry may not be as big as others, but you are doing a great work. You are showing people the love and kindness of God. People are hurting and need help. God is using you to be a blessing in someone's life. Years ago, I was almost homeless and I had to go to many outreach ministries to get food, clothing, toys, gas vouchers, and financial help to pay bills. It was a very humbling experience. People like Tabitha are genuinely making a sacrifice of their time by serving people who are at rock bottom.

Tabitha experienced the supernatural. God used her story for His glory and she was indeed a walking, talking, breathing miracle. God allowed her to suffer momentarily, so He could raise her up and give her a testimony. Looking at her life, we realize that God will get the glory out of what we are going through. When people heard about what happened to Tabitha, they got saved. They couldn't deny the hand of God at work. Being raised from the dead is a sign that the Kingdom has come (Matthew 10:7-8). God wants us to live supernatural lives so others can believe in Jesus. The lost will look at us and want to serve our God.

Tabitha was very creative. God loves to give His people ideas to generate wealth so we can become a blessing and glorify Him. Tabitha had willing hands and she was very productive (Proverbs 31:13). Instead of wasting time, Tabitha worked hard on her business. When Apostle Peter came into her room, he was amazing at everything that she had made. He saw the shirts, tunics, coats, robes, garments, and clothing. Tabitha was an entrepreneur and her business allowed her to finance the Kingdom and take care of the poor. She was a woman of sustenance and had no lack. If you are an entrepreneur, God has need of you. There is a need for more Kingdom business on the scenes. There are a few such as Hobby Lobby and Chick-fil-A. They aren't afraid of their faith and Christian values. God makes sure they prosper even though they are closed on Sundays. These businesses donate to many organizations and charities for the glory of God.

Declaration:

I decree that the Lord has given my hands the power to generate wealth (Deuteronomy 8:18). I will prosper and be a blessing to the poor and needy. I will allow the Lord to download creativity in me.

The Story Continues

THE STORY ENDS WITH you continuing the journey. As you can see, these women's lives had significance and greatly impacted others around them. They laid the foundation. Now you can pick up the torch and finish where they left off. Their names may not be mentioned a lot, but they were special in God's sight. You aren't insignificant, but you are chosen, called, and equipped to do what God is calling you to do. Look at the list below and circle the attributes that you possess. You will be surprised at how many great qualities you carry.

- Dealing with difficult people

- Saving lives
- Wisdom
- Quick thinker, moved swiftly
- Discerning
- Beautiful
- Kind
- Humble
- Strength
- Favor
- Boldness
- Servant
- Trusting God for vindication
- Patience
- Spirit-filled
- Faith
- Conflict management
- Repentant heart
- Brave
- Risk Taker
- Caretaker
- Financial supporter
- Justice
- Endurance
- Confident
- Business mogul
- Worshipper

- Yielded
- Hard worker
- Respected
- Doesn't drink too much wine
- Not greedy
- Blameless
- Self-controlled
- Trustworthy
- Non-gossipper
- Be the wife of one husband
- Rule households well
- Mentor
- Reverence for the Lord
- Good decision making
- Great management
- Giver
- Give alms
- Experienced the miraculous
- Creativity

I am a significant woman that God has set apart to do great exploits on this earth. People may have counted me out, but God has counted me in. There are more positive things about me than negative. I will leave a lasting impact on the next generation!

About The Author

KIMBERLY MOSES STARTED OFF her ministry as Kimberly Hargraves. She is highly sought after as a prophetic voice, intercessor and prolific author. There is no doubt that she has a global mandate on her life to serve the nations of the world by spreading the Gospel of Jesus Christ. She has a quickly expanding worldwide healing and deliverance ministry. Kimberly Moses wears many hats to fulfill the call God has placed on her life as an entrepreneur over several businesses including her own personal brand Rejoice Essentials which promotes the Gospel of Jesus Christ.

She also serves as a life coach and mentor to many women. She is also the loving mother of two wonderful children. She is married to Tron. Kimberly has dedicated her life to the work of ministry and to serve others under the call God has placed over her life. Kimberly currently resides in South Carolina.

She is a very anointed woman of God who signs, miracles and wonders follow. The miraculous and incessant testimonies attributed to her ministry are incalculable, with many reporting physical and mental healing, financial breakthroughs, debt cancellations and other favorable outcomes. She is known across the globe as a servant who truly labors on behalf of God's people through intercession.

She is the author of The Following:

"Overcoming Difficult Life Experiences with Scriptures and Prayers"
"Overcoming Emotions with Prayers"
"Daily Prayers That Bring Changes"
"In Right Standing,"
"Obedience Is Key,"

"Prayers That Break The Yoke Of The Enemy: A Book Of Declarations,"
"Prayers That Demolish Demonic Strongholds: A Book Of Declarations,"
"Work Smarter. Not Harder. A Book Of Declarations For The Workforce,"
"Set The Captives Free: A Book Of Deliverance."
"Pray More Challenge"
"Walk By Faith: A Daily Devotional"
"Empowering The New Me: Fifty Tips To Becoming A Godly Woman"
"School of the Prophets: A Curriculum For Success"
"8 Keys To Accessing The Supernatural"
"Conquering The Mind: A Daily Devotional"
"Enhancing The Prophetic In You"
"The ABCs of The Prophetic: Prophetic Characteristics"
"Wisdom Is The Principal Thing: A Daily Devotional"
"It Cost Me Everything"
"The Making Of A Prophet: Women Walking in Prophetic Destiny"
"The Art of Meditation: A Daily Devotional"
"Warfare Strategies: Biblical Weapons"
"Becoming A Better You"

"I Almost Died"
"The Pastor's Secret: The D.L. Series"
"June Bug The Busy Bee: The Gamer"
"June Bug The Busy Bee: The Bully"
"The Weary Prophet: Providing Practical Steps For Restoration"

You can find more about Kimberly at
www.kimberlyhargraves.com

For Rejoice Essential Magazine, visit
www.rejoiceessential.com

For beauty and t-shirts, visit
www.rejoicingbeauty.com

Please write a review for my books on Amazon.com

Support this ministry:
Cashapp: $ProphetessKim
Paypal.me/remag

References

1. "H26 - 'Abiygayil - Strong's Hebrew Lexicon (KJV)." Blue Letter Bible. Accessed 18 Oct, 2020. https://www.blueletterbible.org//lang/lexicon/lexicon.cfm?Strongs=H26&t=KJV
2. "H5037 - Nabal - Strong's Hebrew Lexicon (KJV)." Blue Letter Bible. Accessed 18 Oct, 2020. https://www.blueletterbible.org//lang/lexicon/lexicon.cfm?Strongs=H5037&t=KJV
3. "H49 - 'Abiyshag - Strong's Hebrew Lexicon (KJV)." Blue Letter Bible. Accessed 18 Oct, 2020. https://www.blueletterbible.org//lang/lexicon/lexicon.cfm?Strongs=H49&t=KJV
4. "H5915 - `Akcah - Strong's Hebrew Lexicon (KJV)." Blue Letter Bible. Accessed 18 Oct, 2020. https://www.bluelet-

terbible.org//lang/lexicon/lexicon.cfm?Strongs=H5915&t=KJV

5. "H1090 - Bilhah - Strong's Hebrew Lexicon (KJV)." Blue Letter Bible. Accessed 18 Oct, 2020. https://www.blueletterbible.org//lang/lexicon/lexicon.cfm?Strongs=H1090&t=KJV
6. "H1783 - Diynah - Strong's Hebrew Lexicon (KJV)." Blue Letter Bible. Accessed 18 Oct, 2020. https://www.blueletterbible.org//lang/lexicon/lexicon.cfm?Strongs=H1783&t=KJV
7. "G1665 - elisabet - Strong's Greek Lexicon (KJV)." Blue Letter Bible. Accessed 18 Oct, 2020. https://www.blueletterbible.org//lang/lexicon/lexicon.cfm?Strongs=G1665&t=KJV
8. "G2131 - eunik - Strong's Greek Lexicon (KJV)." Blue Letter Bible. Accessed 18 Oct, 2020. https://www.blueletterbible.org//lang/lexicon/lexicon.cfm?Strongs=G2131&t=KJV
9. "G3090 - lis - Strong's Greek Lexicon (KJV)." Blue Letter Bible. Accessed 18 Oct, 2020. https://www.bluelet-

terbible.org//lang/lexicon/lexicon.cfm?Strongs=G3090&t=KJV

10. "G2136 - euodia - Strong's Greek Lexicon (KJV)." Blue Letter Bible. Accessed 18 Oct, 2020. https://www.blueletterbible.org//lang/lexicon/lexicon.cfm?Strongs=G2136&t=KJV
11. "G4941 - syntych - Strong's Greek Lexicon (KJV)." Blue Letter Bible. Accessed 18 Oct, 2020. https://www.blueletterbible.org//lang/lexicon/lexicon.cfm?Strongs=G4941&t=KJV
12. "H1904 - Hagar - Strong's Hebrew Lexicon (KJV)." Blue Letter Bible. Accessed 18 Oct, 2020. https://www.blueletterbible.org//lang/lexicon/lexicon.cfm?Strongs=H1904&t=KJV
13. "H3278 - Ya`el - Strong's Hebrew Lexicon (KJV)." Blue Letter Bible. Accessed 18 Oct, 2020. https://www.blueletterbible.org//lang/lexicon/lexicon.cfm?Strongs=H3278&t=KJV
14. "H3089 - Yehowsheba` - Strong's Hebrew Lexicon (KJV)." Blue Letter Bible. Accessed 18 Oct, 2020. https://www.

blueletterbible.org//lang/lexicon/lexicon.cfm?Strongs=H3089&t=KJV

15. "G2490 - ianan - Strong's Greek Lexicon (KJV)." Blue Letter Bible. Accessed 18 Oct, 2020. https://www.blueletterbible.org//lang/lexicon/lexicon.cfm?Strongs=G2490&t=KJV
16. "H3115 - Yowkebed - Strong's Hebrew Lexicon (KJV)." Blue Letter Bible. Accessed 18 Oct, 2020. https://www.blueletterbible.org//lang/lexicon/lexicon.cfm?Strongs=H3115&t=KJV
17. "G2458 - iounias - Strong's Greek Lexicon (KJV)." Blue Letter Bible. Accessed 18 Oct, 2020. https://www.blueletterbible.org//lang/lexicon/lexicon.cfm?Strongs=G2458&t=KJV
18. "H6989 - Qetuwrah - Strong's Hebrew Lexicon (KJV)." Blue Letter Bible. Accessed 18 Oct, 2020. https://www.blueletterbible.org//lang/lexicon/lexicon.cfm?Strongs=H6989&t=KJV
19. "H3865 - Luwd - Strong's Hebrew Lexicon (KJV)." Blue Letter Bible. Accessed 18 Oct, 2020. https://www.bluelet-

terbible.org//lang/lexicon/lexicon.cfm?Strongs=H3865&t=KJV
20. "G4069 - persis - Strong's Greek Lexicon (KJV)." Blue Letter Bible. Accessed 18 Oct, 2020. https://www.blueletterbible.org//lang/lexicon/lexicon.cfm?Strongs=G4069&t=KJV
21. "G5170 - tryphaina - Strong's Greek Lexicon (KJV)." Blue Letter Bible. Accessed 18 Oct, 2020. https://www.blueletterbible.org//lang/lexicon/lexicon.cfm?Strongs=G5170&t=KJV
22. "G5402 - phoib - Strong's Greek Lexicon (KJV)." Blue Letter Bible. Accessed 18 Oct, 2020. https://www.blueletterbible.org//lang/lexicon/lexicon.cfm?Strongs=G5402&t=KJV
23. "G4252 - priskilla - Strong's Greek Lexicon (KJV)." Blue Letter Bible. Accessed 18 Oct, 2020. https://www.blueletterbible.org//lang/lexicon/lexicon.cfm?Strongs=G4252&t=KJV
24. "H6326 - Puw`ah - Strong's Hebrew Lexicon (KJV)." Blue Letter Bible. Accessed 18 Oct, 2020. https://www.bluelet-

terbible.org//lang/lexicon/lexicon.cfm?Strongs=H6326&t=KJV

25. "H8236 - Shiphrah - Strong's Hebrew Lexicon (KJV)." Blue Letter Bible. Accessed 18 Oct, 2020. https://www.blueletterbible.org//lang/lexicon/lexicon.cfm?Strongs=H8236&t=KJV
26. "H7609 - She'erah - Strong's Hebrew Lexicon (KJV)." Blue Letter Bible. Accessed 18 Oct, 2020. https://www.blueletterbible.org//lang/lexicon/lexicon.cfm?Strongs=H7609&t=KJV
27. "G5000 - tabitha - Strong's Greek Lexicon (KJV)." Blue Letter Bible. Accessed 18 Oct, 2020. https://www.blueletterbible.org//lang/lexicon/lexicon.cfm?Strongs=G5000&t=KJV

Index

A

Aaron, 56, 58
Abida, 63
Abigail, 5, 6, 7, 8, 9, 10
Abishag, 12, 14, 15, 17
abortion, 57
Abraham, 42, 43, 63, 64, 65
abundance, 8, 86
accepts, 2
accomplish, 4
accomplished, 40
Achsah, 19, 20, 21, 22
activated, 34
addicted, 68
admonition, 36
Adonijah, 15
adorned, 20
advantage, 16

adversity, 48
Ahaziah, 50
alms, 88, 89, 94
Amnon, 15
Amram, 56
Andronicus, 60
angel, 44, 45
anoint, 48, 54
anointed, 1, 2, 11, 52, 61, 96
anointing, 16
Apollos, 80
Apostles, 53
appointed, 3
Aquila, 78, 79
army, 48
ashamed, 13
assignment, 39, 51, 61, 62, 73, 79
Athaliah, 50, 51
attack, 6, 19
attracted, 14, 15, 28
attractions, 85
attributes, 32, 53, 61, 87, 92
author, 95, 96
avenge, 31
avenged, 29

B

babies, 9, 57, 81
background, 7, 78
backslide, 71
baptized, 66, 68
Barak, 48
bastards, 12
battles, 30
beautiful, 5, 10, 11, 12, 20, 23, 28, 66, 68, 81
Beautiful, 6, 93
beauty, 10, 14, 15, 16, 51, 98
bed chamber, 12
bedroom, 13
believe, 35, 60, 90
believers, 35, 36, 57, 85
benefits, 12, 13
Bible, 1, 4, 5, 14, 20, 26, 29, 32, 35, 36, 38, 39, 42, 47, 50, 53, 56, 60, 63, 66, 70, 71, 72, 74, 78, 81, 84, 87
biblical, 40, 41
Bilhah, 24, 25, 26
birthed, 34, 56
Blameless, 75, 94
bleak, 2
bless, 3, 6, 7, 22, 33, 45, 67, 68, 69, 82, 85

blessing, 22, 23, 43, 65, 69, 86, 89, 90, 91
blood, 41
bloodline, 52
body, 10, 12, 15, 17, 20, 25, 45, 53, 54, 76, 88
bold, 23, 52, 77, 83
Boldness, 21, 76, 93
bossy, 7
Brave, 47, 93
breathing, 9, 17, 72, 90
bright, 74
broken, 16, 28, 29, 71, 80
burial, 53, 54
business, 6, 25, 67, 73, 90, 91
Business mogul, 67, 93
businesses, 85, 91, 95
businesswoman, 66, 85

C

Caleb, 19, 20
called, 2, 12, 40, 54, 64, 75, 76, 87, 92
Caretaker, 54, 93
celebrate, 80
certificates, 10
challenges, 8, 17, 83
Changes, 96

characteristic, 51, 71, 74
characteristics, 6, 10, 17, 21, 56, 67, 78, 84
charitable, 87
charities, 91
cherish, 16
Chick-fil-A, 91
child, 37, 42, 43, 44, 58, 59
children, 9, 12, 24, 26, 36, 37, 42, 58, 59, 67, 96
choice, 7, 48
chosen, 12, 14, 47, 92
Christian, 86, 91
church, 38, 54, 55, 74, 75, 76
client, 7
commandments, 82
commitment, 13
community, 61, 75, 88
companion, 64
companionship, 65
compassionate, 55
compromise, 13
conception, 43
concubine, 12, 13, 14, 24, 63, 65
confidence, 64
Confident, 64, 93
conflict, 39, 40, 41
confusion, 39

connections, 51
conqueror, 52
controlling, 29, 72
conversation, 7, 16
counted, 2, 51, 94
countrymen, 60
courageous, 52
courageousness, 48
covenant, 13
creation, 5
creative, 90
creativity, 91
Creativity, 88, 94
cried, 28, 30, 48
crime, 30
crown, 64, 65
cry, 30
curb, 43
curse, 2, 4

D

Dan, 24
danger, 6
daughter, 19, 23, 28, 50, 51, 57, 58, 84
David, 5, 6, 8, 12, 14, 17

deacon, 75
deaconess, 74, 76
Deborah, 1, 47, 48
debt, 21, 96
deceitful, 75
decision, 84, 85, 94
decisions, 8
Declaration, 11, 18, 23, 27, 31, 34, 37, 41, 46, 49, 52, 55, 59, 62, 65, 69, 73, 76, 80, 83, 86, 91
Declarations, 97
dedicated, 26, 96
delicate, 71
deliver, 30
demon slayer, 49
demonic, 57
demonized, 6
demonstration, 61
depressed, 20
descendants, 45
desert, 43, 44, 45
desired, 22
devil, 40, 52
Difficult, 96
diligence, 73
Dinah, 28, 29, 30
disagreement, 38

discern, 9, 16, 21
Discerning, 6, 93
discernment, 9
disciples, 73
discouraged, 3, 9
discover, 4, 14
distract, 62
distracted, 15
division, 38
dollars, 22
domestic, 19
donate, 91
doors, 3
Dorcas, 87
dormant, 34
dreams, 14, 19, 23
dying, 12, 17

E

ears, 9
earth, 29, 59, 62, 94
education, 14
Egyptian, 81
Eldaah, 63
Elisabeth, 32, 33

embarrassment, 25
Emotions, 96
empower, 4
empty, 3, 25
encounters, 45
encourage, 4, 61
Endurance, 61, 93
endured, 28, 30, 42
enemies, 30
enemy, 7, 38, 48, 50, 52, 62, 83
Enemy, 97
engagement, 2, 75
entertain, 16
entrepreneur, 90, 95
envying, 39
Ephah, 63
Epher, 63
Ephraim, 84
equipped, 92
equipping, 48
era, 44
Ester, 1
eternity, 17
Eunice, 35
Euodia, 38, 40
evil, 39, 47, 50, 57, 59

ex-boyfriend, 28
exhausted, 71
expensive, 67
exploits, 21, 58, 59, 94
extraordinary, 67
eyes, 4, 10, 15, 58, 87

F

faith, 4, 35, 57, 75, 83, 91
Faith, 36, 93, 97
faithful, 3, 20, 66, 77
faithfulness, 3, 32
fame, 23
family, 6, 21, 23, 24, 25, 37, 42, 43, 44, 46, 51, 67
favor, 3, 21, 22, 23, 58
Favor, 21, 56, 93
fear, 29, 36, 82, 83
fellow, 60, 79
female, 60, 61
finances, 54
financial help, 89
Financial supporter, 54, 93
fire, 2, 68, 86
fired, 83
flow, 33, 40, 79

focus, 39, 40, 44
food, 6, 22, 54, 72, 89
fool, 5
forgotten, 2, 26, 33
forsake, 2
foundation, 36, 92
free, 7, 20, 30, 47, 60, 88
friend, 70
frustrated, 3
fulfill, 27, 48, 95
funds, 55
future, 14, 28

G

gatekeepers, 36
generation, 36, 59, 94
Giver, 88, 94
glad, 7
global, 95
glorified, 16
glorify, 40, 90
glory, 3, 48, 56, 65, 89, 90, 91
God, 1, 2, 3, 4, 5, 6, 7, 8, 9, 13, 16, 17, 19, 21, 22, 23, 26, 27, 29, 30, 31, 32, 33, 35, 36, 37, 38, 39, 40, 43, 44, 45, 46, 48, 49, 51, 52, 53, 54, 55, 56,

57, 58, 59, 61, 62, 64, 65, 66, 67, 68, 69, 71, 73, 76, 80, 82, 83, 85, 86, 88, 89, 90, 91, 92, 93,94, 95, 96
good steward, 88
goodness, 45, 82, 86
gorgeous, 10
gospel, 36, 67, 68, 71, 73, 80, 88
graceful, 87
gracious, 53, 64
greedy, 75, 77, 94
Greek, 32, 35, 38, 39, 53, 60, 70, 71, 74, 78, 87

H

Hagar, 42, 43, 44, 45
handiwork, 40
Hanoch, 63
Hard worker, 71, 94
hardships, 61, 62
harsh, 5, 6, 44
harvest, 55, 68, 72, 73
hate, 39
heal, 16, 31
healthcare, 8, 17, 83
heart, 23, 27, 43, 65, 66, 67, 68, 89, 93
heartache, 58, 64, 79

heaven, 72, 73
Heber, 47
Hebrew, 5, 14, 20, 26, 29, 42, 47, 50, 56, 57, 63, 66, 81, 82, 84
help, 5, 19, 30, 40, 44, 48, 54, 58, 71, 79, 85, 89
helpmate, 79
hinder, 62
history, 65
Hobby Lobby, 91
Holy Spirit, 23, 33, 34, 75, 79
home, 36, 54, 68, 69, 79, 80
honored, 22, 58
hoped, 29
horrific, 28, 30
household, 66, 68, 69
households, 76, 94
humble, 17, 18, 43
Humble, 17, 93
humbling, 17, 89
hurt, 31, 83
hurting, 89
husband, 7, 12, 13, 16, 19, 20, 24, 28, 42, 50, 63, 64, 65, 76, 78, 79, 94
husbands, 14, 22, 26, 79

I

illegitimate, 12
immovable, 49
impact, 34, 94
imparting, 36
importance, 4
important, 4, 7, 40, 76, 88
increase, 85
influence, 3
inheritance, 13, 22, 23
insignificant, 1, 2, 3, 4, 17, 58, 92
intercessor, 95
intimacy, 28
intimately, 12
intimidated, 49, 64, 65, 80
invite, 16
Ishmael, 44
Ismael, 42, 43, 44
Israelites, 47, 48

J

Jacob, 20, 24, 25, 28, 30
Jael, 47, 48
jealous, 29, 40, 45, 79
jealousy, 39

Jehoiada, 50, 51
Jehoram, 50, 51
Jehovah, 50
Jehu, 50
Jesus, 2, 25, 26, 32, 33, 35, 49, 50, 52, 53, 54, 57, 59, 61, 62, 72, 73, 77, 80, 87, 88, 90, 95
Jew, 60
Joanna, 53
Joash, 50, 51
job, 17, 44
Jochebed, 56, 57, 58
John the Baptist, 32, 33
Joshua, 19, 22
journey, 4, 24, 61, 64, 76, 92
joy, 5, 64
judged, 30, 66
Judges, 19, 47, 48
judgment, 29
Junia, 60, 61, 62
justice, 30, 57
Justice, 56, 93

K

Keturah, 63, 64, 65
kids, 44

killing, 30, 57
kind, 9, 10, 11, 17, 18, 22, 55, 77, 85
Kind, 17, 75, 93
kingdom builder, 85
Kingdom of Heaven, 59
kinswoman, 84
knowledgeable, 80

L

Laban, 24
laborer, 73
lacked, 79
leader, 75, 76
leadership, 75
Leah, 24, 28
learn, 39, 45, 57, 82
legitimate, 51
Levi, 30
life, 2, 3, 4, 8, 10, 13, 16, 17, 22, 24, 26, 27, 36, 42, 45, 46, 51, 58, 65, 68, 69, 80, 86, 89, 90, 95, 96
lives, 4, 6, 7, 9, 14, 26, 39, 49, 50, 90, 92, 93
Lois, 35
lonely, 25, 64

Lord, 2, 4, 5, 14, 16, 19, 27, 30, 31, 32, 33, 35, 36, 37, 42, 44, 45, 46, 48, 52, 54, 57, 59, 61, 62, 64, 66, 67, 68, 69, 70, 71, 72, 73, 76, 79, 81, 82, 83, 86, 89, 91, 94
lost, 28, 65, 71, 90
love, 20, 25, 29, 41, 55, 59, 64, 65, 89
luxurious, 71

M

maintenance, 88
man, 12, 13, 14, 15, 16, 19, 20, 25, 29, 48, 55, 57, 80, 82
management, 39, 84, 85, 93, 94
mantle, 48
marriage, 20, 23
married, 4, 13, 22, 35, 47, 51, 56, 63, 65, 78, 96
marry, 20, 29
marrying, 14, 19
Mary, 1, 32, 33
masses, 3
masterpiece, 4
mean, 5, 6, 71, 87
meaningless, 1
Mentor, 94
mentoring, 39, 80

mentors, 80
message, 16, 39, 44
Messiah, 33, 80
Mind, 97
minister, 16, 64, 72
ministering, 68, 71
Ministers, 71
ministry, 2, 3, 6, 9, 53, 54, 55, 61, 71, 72, 75, 78, 79, 80, 88, 89, 95, 96, 98
Ministry, 71
miracle, 33, 90
miracles, 96
miraculous, 88, 94, 96
Miriam, 56, 57, 58
miserable, 29
mistress, 25, 43, 44, 45
modestly, 15
money, 22, 54, 55, 85, 88
Moses, 56, 58, 95
mother, 9, 32, 35, 42, 45, 56, 96
motivated, 19
mourning, 89
mouth, 8

N

Nabal, 5, 6
names, 1, 65, 71, 87, 92
Naphtali, 24
nation, 44
nations, 34, 45, 86, 95
Nebuchadnezzar, 57
needy, 89, 91
negative, 94
Non-gossipper, 76, 94
notoriety, 54

O

oath, 32, 50
obedience, 69
Obedience, 96
offense, 40
office, 61, 62, 76
organizations, 85, 91
orphans, 89

P

pain, 17, 28, 29
pastor, 75
pastors, 15

patience, 6
Patience, 33, 93
patient, 6, 8, 9, 11, 33
Paul, 36, 38, 61, 66, 68, 70, 74, 78
peace, 6, 7, 38, 40, 64, 65
peaceful, 79
peacemakers, 40
persecution, 61
persecutors, 62
Persis, 70, 72
person, 5, 17, 39, 40, 86
personalities, 6
personality, 65
persuaded, 66
pest, 7
Peter, 87, 90
Pharaoh, 56, 58, 81, 82
Phoebe, 74, 75, 76
plans, 7, 73
pleasure, 12
plentiful, 73
poor, 89, 90, 91
position, 44, 51, 61, 65, 89
positive, 36, 37, 94
possession, 15
powerfully, 1

powerhouse, 34
powerless, 1
pray, 7, 8, 9, 30, 31, 37, 40, 41, 59, 72, 73
prayers, 7, 23, 36
preach, 3, 16, 40
preaching, 3, 71, 75, 79, 88
pregnant, 4, 32, 33, 43
presence, 29, 68
present, 17, 30
pretty, 7, 14
prevail, 80
prey, 43
prideful, 7, 43
priority, 12
Priscilla, 78, 79, 80
prisoners, 60
prize, 19
profit, 67
profitable, 85
prominent, 78
promiscuous, 20
promise, 32, 33, 42, 43, 45
promises, 27, 33
promoter, 3
promotion, 2
property, 13, 24, 85

prophecy, 49
prophesy, 33
prophetic, 5, 49, 56, 95
prophets, 22, 56
Prophets, 97
prosper, 21, 23, 83, 91
prospered, 8
prostitute, 30
protect, 83
protection, 57, 83
protector, 27
provider, 27
provision, 46, 83
Puah, 81, 82
pulpit, 15, 71
purpose, 4, 14

Q

qualifications, 75
qualities, 4, 17, 40, 92
quit, 2

R

Rachel, 20, 24, 25

radiant, 74
rapist, 29
rebuked, 39
recognition, 54
refreshed, 64
refusal, 83
refute, 16, 62
rejected, 1, 2
rejection, 16
relationships, 16
remarried, 63
repent, 46
repentance, 33
resources, 54, 55, 71
Respected, 75, 94
restore, 31
Reuben, 25, 26
revelation, 62
Reverence, 82, 94
reward, 55, 69, 73, 76, 79
Rhema, 72
rich, 73
riches, 23
righteously, 31
righteousness, 59
Risk Taker, 51, 93

rock bottom, 85, 89
roots, 36
rottenness, 64
royal heirs, 50
Ruth, 1

S

sabotage, 52
sacrifice, 43, 58, 59, 89
safe, 9
salvation, 35
Sarah, 42, 43, 44, 45, 63, 64
satisfied, 23
scandal, 41
Scriptures, 80, 96
self-controlled, 77
Self-controlled, 75, 94
selfish, 5
selfless, 55
servant, 24, 25, 26, 27, 74, 77, 96
Servant, 26, 93
servants, 8, 48, 69, 71
serving, 26, 57, 75, 89
sex, 12, 13, 14, 15, 18
shame, 25, 29, 64

Shechem, 28, 29, 30
Sheerah, 84, 85, 86
Shiphrah, 81, 82
significant, 26, 58, 73, 94
signs, 16, 61, 96
Simeon, 30
sin, 7
sinning, 82
Sisera, 47, 48
sister, 15, 24, 30, 74
situation, 7, 30
slave, 42, 44, 60
social status, 12
Solomon, 15
soul winner, 73
South Carolina, 96
sow, 40
sower, 55
spirit, 7, 33, 43, 52, 60, 67, 68
Spirit of God, 48
Spirit-filled, 33, 52, 93
spiritual gifts, 33, 34
splendid, 81
stages, 17
story, 5, 6, 7, 12, 17, 19, 20, 21, 26, 28, 32, 38, 42, 47, 50, 51, 56, 76, 81, 87, 89, 92

stranger, 28, 42
strategies, 21, 68
strength, 18
Strength, 17, 93
strengthen, 49
stretch marks, 10
strife, 39, 66
Strongholds, 97
successful, 66
suffered, 30
suicide, 7, 71
Sundays, 91
supernatural, 36, 45, 54, 89, 90
supplies, 6, 8, 72
support, 3, 55, 75, 80
supporter, 53, 54, 78
survive, 21, 45
sustenance, 90
sympathize, 31
synagogue, 80
Syntyche, 38, 40

T

Tabitha, 87, 88, 89, 90
Tamar, 15

teachable, 69
team, 78
territory, 48, 71
tested, 83
testimonies, 96
testimony, 7, 90
thank, 59
throne, 15, 51
time, 2, 3, 6, 7, 8, 10, 12, 19, 21, 25, 28, 30, 32, 33, 36, 40, 68, 71, 72, 89, 90
Timothy, 35, 36, 75
title, 7, 61, 76
titles, 62
tough, 6
tourists, 85
transportation, 85
trauma, 31
treasure, 9, 23
treasures, 14
trials, 30
tribes, 26
Tron, 96
trophy, 14, 18
trouble, 30, 83
trust, 30, 31, 55, 83
Trusting, 93

trustworthy, 77
Trustworthy, 76, 94
Tryphena, 70, 72
Tryphosa, 70, 71, 72

U

unction, 23
unimportant, 1
unselfishness, 55
unshakeable, 49
untraceable, 52

V

vain, 69
value, 9, 11, 13
Vengeance, 31
victory, 35
vindicated, 29, 30, 40
vindication, 29, 31, 93
violated, 29
virginity, 28
virtue, 18
virtuous, 19
vision, 2, 8, 40, 44, 61, 72

visitation, 45
voice, 3, 8, 9, 21, 68, 95
vow, 32

W

war, 19, 20, 49, 52
warriors, 36
wealth, 21, 86, 88, 89, 90, 91
wealthy, 5
weapon, 52
weapons, 83
weary, 33
Weeping, 64
whole, 24, 31
wicked, 51, 56
wickedness, 51
widows, 89
wife, 5, 12, 13, 15, 19, 21, 24, 32, 42, 50, 53, 63, 64, 65, 76, 78, 94
wifey, 19
wilderness, 23, 33, 45
wine, 75, 94
Wisdom, 6, 21, 93, 97
wise, 11, 72
wives, 12, 25, 79

woman, 11, 12, 18, 26, 32, 47, 48, 55, 58, 64, 65, 66, 70, 75, 83, 86, 87, 88, 90, 94, 96
womb, 32, 33
women, 1, 4, 10, 13, 14, 16, 19, 22, 35, 36, 38, 39, 48, 53, 61, 70, 71, 72, 79, 81, 82, 92, 96
wonders, 16, 61, 96
world, 1, 10, 20, 25, 30, 36, 57, 63, 95
worry, 2, 62
worship, 54, 68
worshipped, 66
Worshipper, 67, 93
worth, 11, 15, 16, 20, 23, 83
wounds, 16, 54
wrath, 31

Y

Yahweh, 50
yield, 69, 79
Yielded, 67, 94

Z

Zechariah, 3, 32

Made in the USA
Middletown, DE
08 November 2022

14409017R00086